To my friends at St. John the Evangelist C[hurch]

Msgr. Hayes
Father Paul
Father Fred

A book is twice enjoyed when shared with another

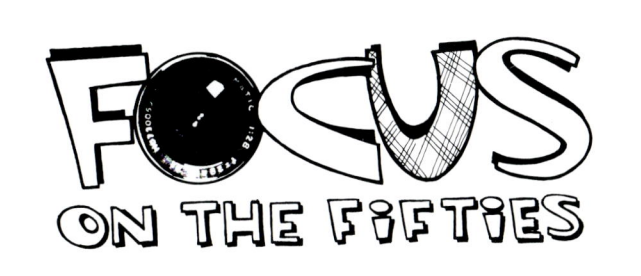

FOCUS
ON THE FIFTIES

The passing years brought few changes to the imposing structure of the First Church of Christ, Scientist, the future home of the Oneida County Historical Society at 1608 Genesee Street, corner of Avery Place, in Utica.
12/21/59 33479

FOCUS ON THE FIFTIES
UTICA AND VICINITY, 1950-1962

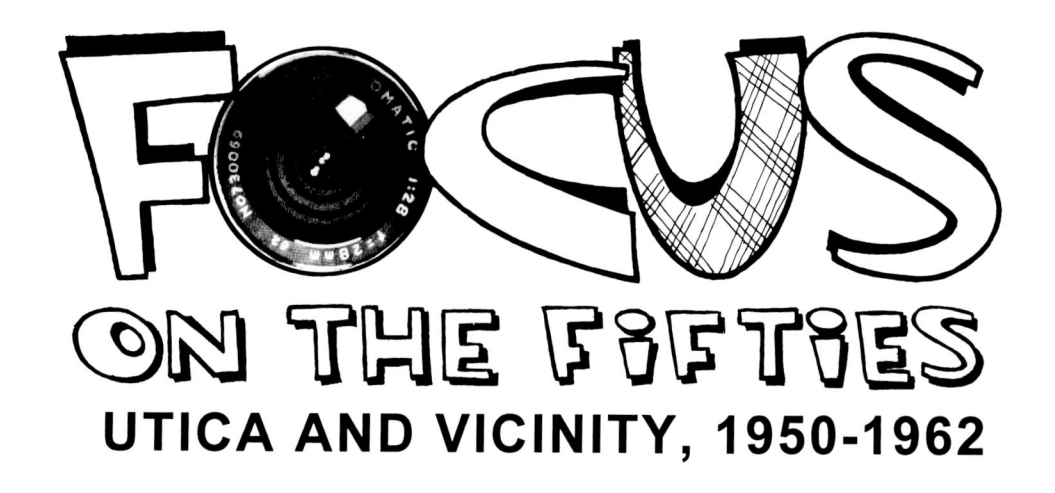

More Photographs from the Russell Rhoades Collection

Compiled by Eleanor "Peg" Hassett

Additional material by Douglas M. Preston

ONEIDA COUNTY HISTORICAL SOCIETY
UTICA, NEW YORK

NORTH COUNTRY BOOKS, INC.
Utica, New York

FOCUS ON THE FIFTIES
UTICA AND VICINITY, 1950-1962

More Photographs from the
Russell Rhoades Collection

Copyright © 1995
by
Oneida County Historical Society
Utica, New York

All Rights Reserved

No part of this book may be reproduced
in any manner without written
permission of the publisher.

ISBN 0-925168-44-0

Library of Congress Cataloging-in-Publication Data

Hassett, Eleanor, 1917-
    Focus on the fifties Utica and vicinity, 1950-1962.
       p. cm.
    ISBN 0-925168-43-2 (cloth : alk. paper),
    ISBN 0-925168-44-0 (pbk. : alk. paper)
    1. Utica (N.Y.)—Pictorial works.
F129.U8H35   1995
974.7'62—dc20   95-36088
                                            CIP

Published by
NORTH COUNTRY BOOKS, INC.
PUBLSIHER—DISTRIBUTOR
311 Turner Street
Utica, New York 13501

Dedicated to
David Maldwyn Ellis
Oneida County Historical Society Fellow
Board Member
Past President
Premier Historian of New York State
and
Our Friend

Russell T. Rhoades, 1936

" . . . photographs link us to our past by making it tangible. In doing so they speak directly to our hearts, and they have a power and a significance that make them a precious element of our heritage."

> William F. Stapp
> Former Curator of Photographs
> The National Portrait Gallery
> Smithsonian Institution

Table of Contents

Foreword	8
Introduction	10
Downtown	13
The Neighborhoods	39
The Suburbs and Beyond	61
Home, School and Play	79
Getting There	89
From Loom to Boom	105
Digital Retouching	127
Afterword	128

Foreword

Some of the larger rewards of working for the Oneida County Historical Society come when our offerings are warmly received by the public. When a library patron exclaims, "This is just the information I've been looking for!"; when local residents of all races turn out for the exhibits "Field to Factory: Afro-American Migration 1914-1940" and " 'On the Season': Belle Glade to the Mohawk Valley"; when 300 people crowd into our museum for "An Evening with Walter D. Edmonds," and when would-be buyers still seek copies of *The Upper Mohawk Country: An Illustrated History of Greater Utica* more than a decade after it went out of print, then budget crises and plumbing problems and the occasional difficult visitor are forgotten.

The reception afforded our first volume of Russell Rhoades photos was just such a reward. People literally lined up to buy *Not So Long Ago: Utica and Vicinity 1940-1949* when it appeared just before Christmas 1992. It was a best-seller in local bookstores for several weeks.

The period covered by this new book—1950-1962—is not one most people think of when they hear the word history. And when we speak of *local* history, many of us still think of the Battle of Oriskany and the Erie Canal. Our first Rhoades book dealt with the 1940s, including World War II and the heyday of railroads and two-lane highways. We hope that it reminded readers that their experiences—or those of their parents—are part of history, too. We hope that this book, dealing with the time of the Cold War and the Thruway, will do likewise.

Our first book acknowledged Joseph Skane, president of Russell T. Rhoades & Company, Inc., for donating this wonderful collection. In this volume, we must also note his work as a photographer. Joe Skane learned his craft as a darkroom technician at the old Utica *Observer-Dispatch* just before World War II. His teacher was the late great Dante O. Tranquille, for many years the *O-D*'s chief photographer (and a camera artist deserving of several books of his own).

World War II took Joe to Marine boot camp at Parris Island, South Carolina, where he became a staff photographer for the newly-established *Parris Island Boot*. After the war, he pursued other occupations until the mid-1950s when he hired out to Russell Rhoades, then at 106 Liberty Street. As Rhoades' assistant, he was undoubtedly responsible for a fair share of the later work in this volume.

Following Rhoades' acquisition of the John Barnard Blueprint Company and the move to 27 Devereux Street, the photography side of the business began to decline. Old-time local advertising firms like Moser & Cotins and Bair Advertising and long-time clients like Savage Arms and American Emblem retired, left the city or went out of business. Newer, larger businesses—many not locally owned—such as General Electric and Chicago Pneumatic employed their own staff photographers. Insurance adjusters switched to Polaroids for instant records of crumpled fenders and mangled bumpers. Finally, Rhoades' blueprint, graphic supply and reproduction business prospered to the point that hauling heavy cameras and lights all over town became less critical to the bottom line. By the early 1960s, Rhoades' commercial photography had all but ceased; among the most recent pictures in this book is that of the Boston Store expansion of 1962.

Joe Skane purchased the business from Russell Rhoades in 1968. The founder stayed on for about a year before retiring completely; he died February 11, 1978. In 1994, Joe Skane announced his retirement and sold the firm to John and Ronna Kelly.

I also extend the Society's thanks to two remarkable and generous women without whose efforts the Rhoades negatives would still be gathering dust. Peg Hassett volunteered to help organize the collection in 1985. Little did she know what she was getting into! Since then, not only has she organized this collection, and others, but has authored two books, and given countless slide talks based on her work.

In between, she found time to serve as secretary and president of the Society, during which time we purchased, renovated and moved to our new quarters. She is also active in the American Association of University Women, the Unitarian Universalist Church, the Utica & Mohawk Valley Chapter, National Railway Historical Society, and the Utica Camera Club. She and her "friend" Tom (active in the NRHS and the American Legion) have also made several trips abroad and recently celebrated their golden wedding anniversary. Oh yes, and she nursed Tom through major cardiac surgery.

Helen Ney Best Crouse has been a generous benefactor of the Society for many years. Her first husband—Col. Tharratt Gilbert Best—served the Society as president and she has endowed our reference library—of which the Rhoades Collection is a part—in his memory. Her generosity to the Utica Foundation, Inc. also made possible their 1986 grant to the Society to house, preserve and catalog the Rhoades Collection.

Today, with the B-52s gone from Griffiss Air Force Base, and with local General Electric (presently Lockheed Martin) operations slated for closure, it is well to recall that Utica and Oneida County have survived major economic dislocations in the past. The pictures in this book date from a time when our area was undergoing other important changes, from textile manufacturing to defense industries and installations.

All old pictures offer history lessons, and especially illustrate the relentless march of change (not necessarily progress). These selections from the Rhoades Collections reflect change in everything from the city and suburban landscape, to office equipment and computers, to tastes in interior decoration, fashions and automobiles, to the way boys play baseball.

For some, these photographs will evoke memories, hopefully pleasant. For others, they will be an introduction to the Utica area of their parents' or grandparents' day.

—Doug Preston

Introduction

We are pleased to present this, the second volume of photographs from the files of Russell T. Rhoades & Company, commercial photographers, now in the possession and care of the Oneida County Historical Society. Most of the photos in this book were selected from the years 1950-62. Rediscovered in 1981, the complete collection of more than 10,000 Rhoades' negatives covering the years 1940-62 is a treasure trove of local history.

Reviewing the files of Utica newspapers at the Utica Public Library revealed a potpourri of happenings in Utica during the period covered by this book. Many in this area will remember the '50s as a turbulent era, especially in the realm of local politics and government. The Rhoades Collection reflects none of this, but a few items will help to put the pictures in context.

In 1952, the New York State Holstein Association asked its members to protest the sale of yellow oleo-margarine in an effort to protect the butter market.

In 1953, the Utica area hospitals delivered an average of nine babies a day, a good number but below the average for 1951. When this population started in school, the buildings were bulging, especially in the suburbs where most of the new families lived. In 1960, Whitesboro High School was 300 pupils over capacity, and elementary pupils were bussed to a variety of rented rooms. New Hartford and Clinton schools were considering double sessions for some grades.

In August 1955, seven of every ten eligible children in the area received the Salk vaccine, but 25 cases of polio were reported in Oneida, Herkimer and Madison counties.

In November 1957, three Utica residents were found at a meeting of organized-crime leaders in Apalachin. They said they were visiting a sick friend.

In 1959, the Utica papers received a Pulitzer prize for reporting on local crime and graft. It was a first for an upstate New York paper.

In 1960, the new art museum of Munson-Williams-Proctor Institute opened to high praise for the design by Philip Johnson.

In 1962, Robert Fisher, special investigator for the State of New York, closed his office. He and his staff had been investigating irregularities in city and county government.

We found significant differences in the collection in the later years. The emphasis in this period was on industrial scenes and advertising material, with fewer crumpled fenders and other miscellaneous subjects found in the earlier files.

There were more small negatives with multiple views of a single assignment, and because of faster film, many of these showed people at work or play. There were also many more damaged negatives as a result of fires and floods in neighboring buildings which started an irreversible process of decomposition in the negatives. As if to compensate, there were more original prints in good condition.

We were fortunate to find Theresa Sokolowski, owner of Visual Designs, and Dr. Robert Dell of Mohawk Valley Community College who developed a new application of computer digitization, allowing us to use many photos that would otherwise be too damaged. Their work was funded by a grant from Light Work, a community darkroom connected with Syracuse University. The process has great promise for the restoration of faded or torn prints. To our delight, we were able to include some scenes prior to 1950 which were too damaged to use in the first book. All digitized photos are identified in the captions.

We also thank others who aided in the work. Art Lane's skill in the Society's darkroom was much appreciated. Volunteers George and Bea White, Dan Batchelor, Marge Donato, Marge Freytag, Charlie Miller, and Floyd Smith all helped identify scenes. Dick Aversa furnished the picture of Russell Rhoades; Frank Lorenz provided data on Hamilton College and supplied the photo of David Ellis; Bart Rasmus identified old cars; Ralph Shanks helped with Utica Drop Forge, and Albert Treen filled us in on the Waterville Crematory. The reference room staff at the Utica Public Library was very helpful. We would also like to thank Sharron Yoxall for her typing.

We hope that you will enjoy this second volume.

—Peg Hassett

From 1918 until 1958, Liggett's Drug Store was a fixture at or near the Busy Corner where Lafayette joins Genesee Street. This Art Deco building replaced the old Utica Trust & Deposit Company about 1932.
2/12/58   33000

Downtown

Downtown Utica was a busy place. In 1950, the city had a population of 106,000 according to the national census. Mayor Boyd Golder was starting his fifth year in office and the Democrats were firmly in control of the city government.

In 1960, the population was 100,007. Republican Frank Dulan was sworn in for his first term on January 1. The police department was undergoing a reorganization in the wake of devastating disclosures made before and during the investigation headed by Robert Fisher. About thirty Hamilton College students picketed Woolworth's to protest segregation in the southern states. In September, more than 3,000 people gathered at the Memorial Auditorium to greet presidential candidate John F. Kennedy.

Just a short block away from the Busy Corner, the Hotel Utica was the city's finest and a meeting place for residents as well as visitors. It boasted 350 rooms.
2/28/52   29439

The hotel bar was the setting for photos to promote a New York State wine. The local firm of Moser & Cotins was directing the advertising campaign.
3/3/52   29502

The desk in the lobby was the nerve center of the hotel. In 1951, Paul Nonay, a Hungarian displaced person, completed a mural depicting the history of Utica for display in the lobby.
2/15/52   29386

Murals show again in this Hotel Utica photo of a group from Bossert's. The men enjoyed after-dinner cigars, while the woman smiled bravely.
11/8/54   31707 (digitally restored)

15

As late as 1962, the Boston Store showed its confidence in downtown Utica by extending the store to the full block between Oriskany and Bleecker Streets. This was among the last photographs taken by Rhoades.
6/62   33799

Here the Rhoades organization turned to fashion photography.
4/27/62   33786 A

4/27/62   33786 B

In the late '40s, the Boston Store annexed the former Colonial Theater on Bleecker Street. It was later replaced with a new parking garage and furniture department.
5/22/57   32794 (digitally restored)

Across Franklin Square was this well-known men's store. Like many of the buildings on Genesee Street, it had a new store front but the upper floors betrayed its age.
4/16/52   29569

17

Many small shops occupied the building at 126-130 Genesee Street between Liberty and Oriskany Streets; the popular Imperial Restaurant was around the corner. The Flxible bus of the Utica-Old Forge Transit Company stopped here to pick up passengers.
4/16/52   29570

This was Liberty Street looking toward Genesee. The historic old Mechanics Hall occupied the corner of Hotel Street, at left. All of the buildings at right were removed in the 1960s for the East-West Arterial.
6/19/56   32401

At 12 Liberty Street, Colerick Supply Company had a variety of interesting industrial and building equipment. The newer fluorescent lights hung from the old tin ceiling.
5/21/52   29722

One of Utica's oldest neighborhoods, the triangle bounded by Genesee, Whitesboro and Liberty Streets in the Second Ward had been home to Jewish, Polish and other immigrants since the turn of the century. Nookie's Delicatessen was noted for such kosher treats as pastrami on rye. There were pickets on the sidewalk at 228 Oriskany Street, but New York Bakery's sign proclaimed that their bakers were not *on strike. All the buildings in the background were taken down for the expansion of Abelove's Linen (later Associated Textile Service). The Niagara Mohawk gasholder at Harbor Point was in the distance.*
10/54   31545

The Rhoades photographers were able to show what a difference a coat of paint could make to this former factory, built in the 19th century on the bank of the Erie Canal by Alfred Munson (founder of the Munson-Williams-Proctor fortune).
3/15/54   31545

2/8/56   32262

21

Intercity buses used this station on Hotel Street between Oriskany and Liberty Streets.
5/57   32793 (digitally restored)

Harry Heiman had a showroom next to the police station on Oriskany Street. For several years, the Utica papers reported that only Plymouths met City Hall's specifications for an L-head engine for police cars. The spire of Grace Church shows in the background.
6/19/53   30587 H

On Lafayette Street, the Hotel Pershing (built in 1919) adjoined the Hotel Utica (built seven years earlier). In 1954, new owners changed the Pershing's name to the Earle Hotel and promised to correct the substandard plumbing.
8/16/54   31344 A

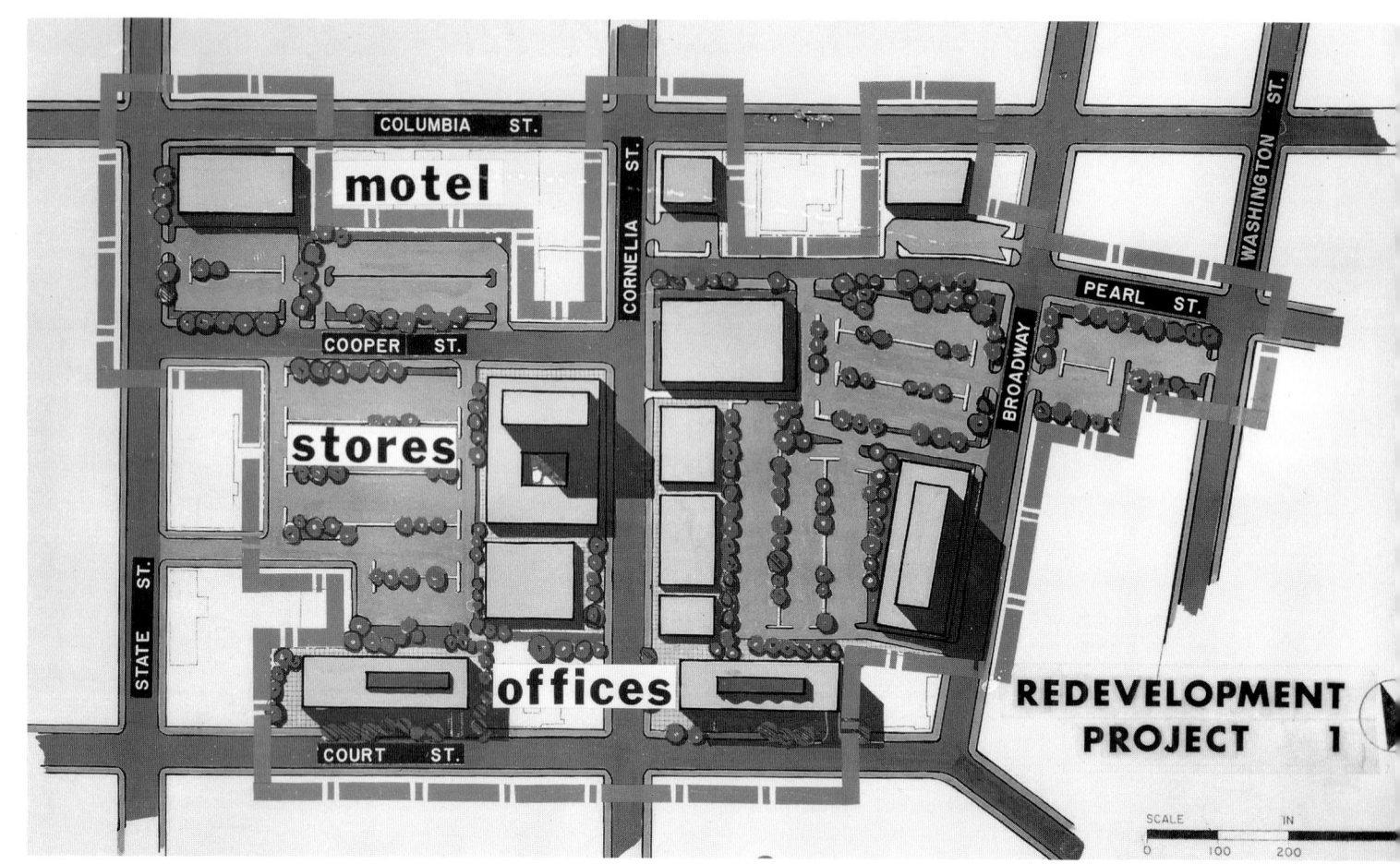

This was one of the many schemes put forth for Urban Renewal Area #1 which consisted of 22.3 acres of land west of City Hall, loosely bounded by Court, State and Columbia Streets. It was planned to demolish 140 housing units and relocate 300 families. Federal funds were available for the project. Retailers protested any plans to put a shopping center in the area, calling it another intrusion into a private enterprise field with public money. They stated that parking was the problem downtown, not lack of stores.
12/23/59   33572

12/15/61   33744 A

12/15/61   33744 B

Lee Electrical Company on the corner of Broadway and Pearl Street was one of many businesses displaced by the Urban Renewal demolition. In the top photo, the spires of Bethesda Congregational and Westminster Presbyterian Churches show; in the middle scene, an apartment building on Pearl Street can be seen; below is the sales counter.
12/15/61   33744 C

Down on lower Genesee Street, Commercial Travelers Insurance Company invested in a new IBM installation to help track accounts. It was definitely not a "laptop" operation.
10/8/57   32895 A

10/8/57   32895 B

In spite of dire predictions about the takeover by the "boob tube," the record business was booming and Woolworth's had the latest hits on LPs or 45s.
5/23/58   33058

11/29/56   32550 A

Here are two views of Bleecker Street taken from the same spot in front of Jones and Gurley Paint Store at 315-317 Bleecker Street opposite Chancellor Park. The top view is looking east, the other to the west.
11/29/56   32550 B

With all the interest in home ownership during this period, everyone wanted to keep up their property. Jones and Gurley was glad to help them with the necessary supplies.
10/21/55   32116 A

The shadow of the spire of Grace Episcopal Church was cast by the late afternoon sun on Utica's tallest structure, the First National Bank Building on the corner of Elizabeth and Genesee Streets.
9/18/62   33830

Many Uticans will remember the old Avon Theater at 212 Lafayette Street. It was one of several downtown movie houses.
12/12/57   32957

In 1954, the stockholders of the First Bank and Trust Company voted shares to Marine Midland Corporation by a large margin. Marine Midland expansion plans called for removal of this steel and glass addition on Seneca Street, first occupied by Homestead Savings & Loan.
2/18/60   33520 A

10/26/56   32530 A

Here are two views of the Mayro Building at Bank Place and Genesee Street. In the lower view from Union Street the dome of the Savings Bank and the tower of City Hall are seen.
10/26/56   32530 B

The Liberty Lodge of Masons gathered at the decorative entrance of the Masonic Temple on Genesee Street for a collective portrait.
5/19/51   28628

The Christian Science Reading Room and several small shops occupied the Albert Hotel next to the Masonic Temple.
7/7/61   33677 A

33

Grant's Book Shop, the mecca for bibliophiles at Genesee and Hopper Streets, had books—lots of them—but much more to keep graduates interested in a lifetime of learning.
12/8/60   33584

In 1953, the intersection of Genesee, Hopper and Court Streets was called the worst in the city. Over 2,700 cars passed here during the evening rush hour.
7/47   23088

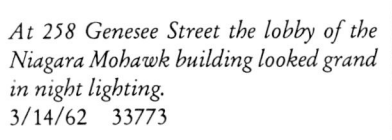

At 258 Genesee Street the lobby of the Niagara Mohawk building looked grand in night lighting.
3/14/62   33773

A couple blocks to the east on Charlotte Street, near the county buildings, the Red Cherry Pie Shop was conveniently located for dessert lovers.
12/3/56   32511 (digitally restored)

Wilcox Jewelers occupied this relatively modest shop at 250 Genesee Street next to the YMCA before moving north to the former Mohawk Valley Investment Company building in 1961.
11/6/60   33574

2/24/57   32683

Cornhill Savings and Loan moved into a bright new building at 266 Genesee Street in 1957. The many teller stations indicated expanding services.
2/16/57   32663 F

South Street was a principal business street of Cornhill. This view looks west from the corner of Miller Street. Preston's Drug Store was noted for good ice cream at the soda fountain.
10/8/57   32896

The Neighborhoods

With the coming of the more affluent '50s, most families had at least one car and many had two. Automobiles expanded the neighborhoods as people were no longer tied to bus routes.

The move to the suburbs began in earnest. In searching for a house, the size of the garage became as important as the number of bedrooms. Homes without a garage or even parking space lost value. The older neighborhoods became areas where less affluent Uticans, displaced by arterials and Urban Renewal, went to live.

However, the old names such as East Utica, Cornhill and the Highlands still clung to sections of the city. Most of these areas had some kind of manufacturing plant in them or nearby and there were always small clusters of shops. But it was not yet possible to fill the gas tank *and* buy milk and bread at the same "convenience" store.

Trinity Evangelical Lutheran Church was one of the first congregations to build on upper Genesee Street. This attractive modern structure is on the former Harter property. Saints Peter and Paul Ukrainian Orthodox Church moved into their former building on Hamilton Street in the historically German neighborhood of West Utica.
10/17/58   33173

Calvary Episcopal Church was built in 1872 on the corner of South Street and Howard Avenue to serve the growing Cornhill area. This traditional gothic building, shaded by one of Utica's many elm trees, was being renovated when this picture was taken. The elm trees along the city streets were being sprayed with DDT in a futile effort to stop Dutch elm beetles.
7/21/60   33520

Children of the congregation of Temple Beth El at Genesee and Scott Streets show some of the features of the building, including the entrance, the bimah at the front of the sanctuary, the Torah, and one of the lovely stained glass windows.
6/58   33087 A, B, C & D

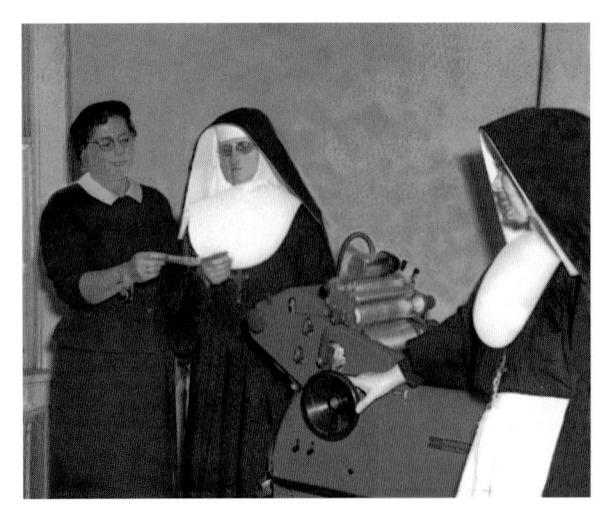

The Sisters of St. Francis were in charge of St. Elizabeth Hospital and were a familiar sight in its corridors and rooms in their traditional habits.
10/4/55   32103 (digitally restored)

Expansive lawns separated the buildings of St. Elizabeth Hospital from upper Genesee Street. In 1950, the average person expected to be a hospital bed patient once every eight years. Twenty-five percent of the population expected to be an out-patient every year.
8/9/51   28858

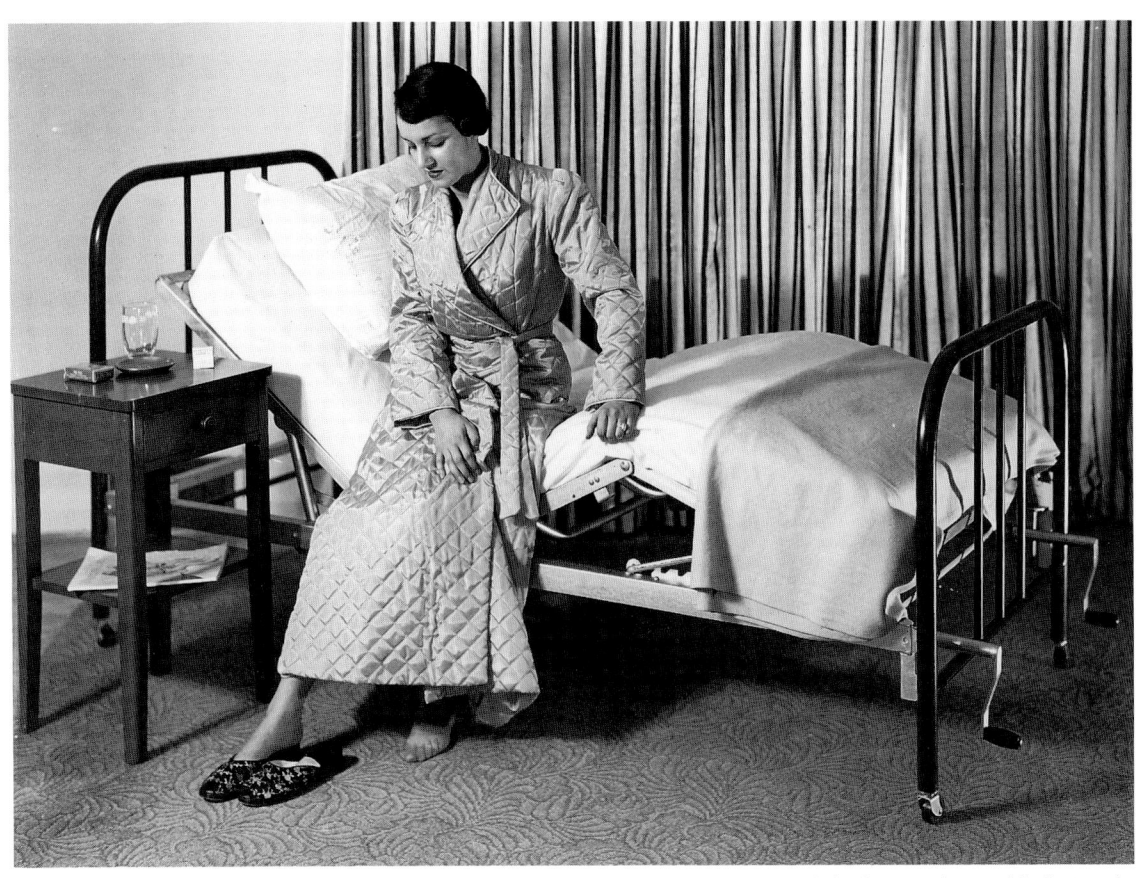

Foster Brothers manufactured the latest in hospital beds. People turning cranks made the adjustments rather than electricity.
10/9/51   29029

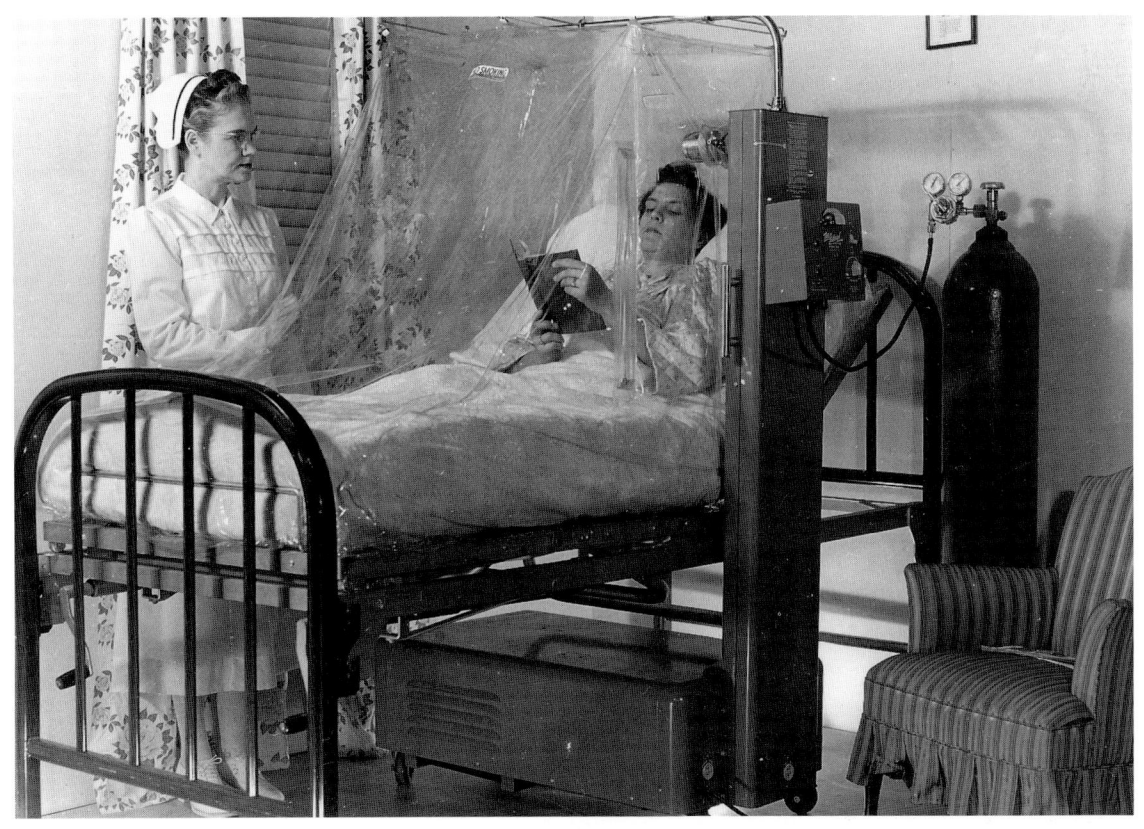

When oxygen was needed, the A. H. St. Louis Company provided it. It's hard to imagine enjoying a novel under such circumstances.
1/19/52   29313

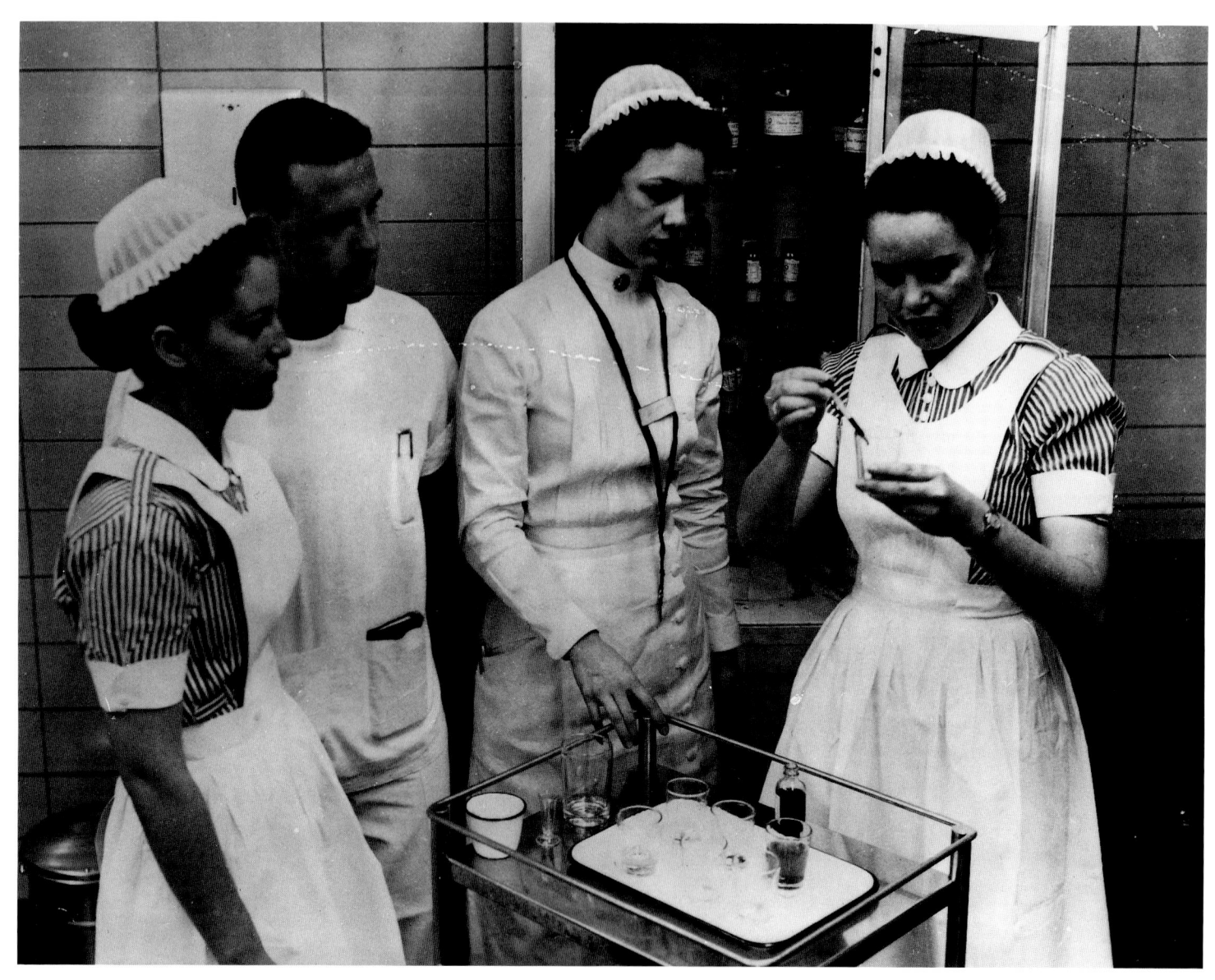

Registered Nurses still wore traditional starched white uniforms which clearly indicated their professional status and caps and pins which identified the schools in which they had taken their training. Here student nurses in striped uniforms were instructed in testing procedures.
1/6/61   33600

St. Luke's Hospital moved into a beautiful new $3.8 million dollar building on Champlin Avenue just outside the city limits, leaving their quarters on Whitesboro Street to be later developed into offices and apartments. Ample parking was a prominent feature of the new location.
7/57   32884

Mahanna Brothers Drug Store on Whitesboro Street served the needs of the residents in the Highlands.
7/24/56   32431 (digitally restored)

Pool and beach gear, cookies and candy, prescriptions and a lunch counter were among the features at Mahanna's.
7/22/56   33431 B

The owner of the former Globe Woolen Mill was seeking a tenant for this huge complex. Later, the State University Institute of Technology ("Upper Division College") occupied this building until the Marcy campus was ready.
2/6/59   33267

West End Brewery was adding on to increase capacity. This view is looking west toward the Utica State Hospital, later Mohawk Valley Psychiatric Center. The tall chimneys were part of the hospital's heating plant.
3/19/55   31821

Lincoln Laundry at 1430 Lincoln Avenue had a remodelled building to show off.
6/10/52   29866

This firm on Lafayette Street sold electrical supplies, repaired motors, and contracted for electrical installations. The motor repair shops were on the second and third floors of the former Turn Verein Hall, next door to the modern structure. The Turn Verein was a gymnastic club founded by German immigrants.
9/57   32882 (digitally restored)

The Coca-Cola bottling plant was at 401 Broad Street near Union Station. Originally an elegant residence, the building was completely remodeled in the 1920s.
10/11/57   32894

901 Broad Street was built as a cotton mill, but when the aerospace division of General Electric Company needed more room, the building became a manufacturing center for sophisticated radar for the military and space agencies. The Route 5S Arterial later ran behind the building and the old Erie Canal bed was filled and paved for parking.
12/30/55   32206 (digitally restored)

Syracuse University, seeing the need for a college here, started one in the vicinity of Oneida Square. College Hall on Hart Street was the only structure actually built for Utica College in that area and it became a favorite photo location. Classes were also held in Plymouth Congregational Church, the former Francis Street School, a war surplus "prefab," and other nearby buildings.
8/1/56   32440 (digitally restored)

This aerial view of South Utica was taken earlier than 1950, but once restored we couldn't leave it out! Sunset Avenue is in the foreground with the greenhouses of Brant Brothers prominently shown. Genesee Street runs through the upper third of the picture with the tracks of the West Shore Railroad crossing at a diagonal.

North of the tracks was the former South Utica station; a freight car was parked on a siding. Other landmarks included the "lighthouse" of Tower Esso at Genesee and Parkside Court, upper left, King Cole Ice Cream in the triangular plot at center right, and directly above King Cole, the White Tower (later moved across the street). In 1955, the vacant property at the top became the site of the Grand Union Shopping Center.

6/24/49 26331 (digitally restored)

5/21/51   28617

5/21/51   28620

Van Tine's card shop at Oneida Square was a popular place. The titles of the magazines on the rack indicate the popularity of home ownership and decorating, as well as a vivid interest in the lives of film stars and sports figures.
5/21/51   28619

32121 G

10/15/55   32121 H

People crowded into the new Wittig's restaurant at Oneida Street near the Parkway. This later became the site of Manny's, famous for cheesecake.
10/15/55   32121 I

6/7/55 32015 A

Neighborhood "Mom and Pop" stores had not yet been replaced with chain "convenience" stores. This was Toukatly's at 1152 Seymour Avenue.
6/7/55 32015 B

1/12/56   32229 A

The Greenpoint Grill at Varick and Whitesboro Streets offered patrons hamburgers for 25¢ and hot sausage sandwiches for 35¢ accompanied by the latest hits on the mammoth juke box. Lost to the East-West Arterial in the early '60s, it was representative of many a small neighborhood "bar and grill."
1/12/56   32229 B

The North Utica Dairy at 333 North Genesee Street advertised its wares with an unmistakable sign, but the New York Milk Distributors said the paper bottle was here to stay. Prewar autos such as the 1938 Buick shown here were still common sights, together with newer models like the 1949 Ford behind it.
9/17/52   30001

The Cadillac Hotel at 102 North Genesee Street was the last stop before the recently opened Thruway.
6/12/58   33073 A

6/12/58   33073 B

58

Deerfield Corners was the hub of North Utica, and just the place to advertise the new North Utica Shopping Center. Mayor McKennan officiated at the opening on June 6, 1956. Texaco stations, sheathed in white enamelled metal and trimmed with dark green stripes and bright red stars. were a common sight for many years.
6/26/58   33088

Ye Olde Restaurant—known as Burky's—was on North Genesee Street near the Thruway.
10/8/56   32513 (digitally restored)

Route 69 (Oriskany Boulevard) in Whitesboro has a very different appearance in this photo but can be recognized by the high school building at the left. Hart's Hill is in the background.
6/4/52   29739 A

The Suburbs and Beyond

Some of the larger businesses, notably Utica Mutual Insurance Company, left the city and established headquarters in areas where parking was available. It became less and less necessary to go downtown as shopping centers with huge parking lots opened in New Hartford and Whitesboro as well as in North Utica. The new shopping centers also combined with improved highways to draw shoppers from fifty or more miles away.

Whitestown Shopping Center was just a big field in this photo, but plans were well underway. The sign proclaimed 82% occupancy before construction was started. The tall chimney in the background was of the former Whitestown Seminary, at this time occupied by Kerk Guild, manufacturers of jewelry boxes and other novelties.
6/4/52   29739 B

With the postwar baby boom, new schools had to be built. This was New York Mills, on part of the former site of the World War II Rhoads General Hospital.
6/9/59   33377

The kitchen at the popular Trinkaus Manor restaurant in Oriskany was equipped with Revere pots and pans and made an ideal subject for an advertisement.
2/10/55   31820

Jay-K Lumber was near the point where Route 5, known since the early 1800s as the Seneca Turnpike, joined Route 5A, built in the 1930s and commonly called "the truck route" and later named Commercial Drive.
9/7/53   30886 (digitally restored)

This charming house on Oxford Road in the Village of New Hartford, was later moved to make way for a new fire station. The former firehouse on Park Street can be seen at the right of the top photo and the left of the middle one. The kitchen had been remodelled in then popular knotty pine.
5/20/55   31950 A, B & C

At the new shopping center in New Hartford, where there was parking for 2,500 cars, Woolworth's occupied a large section.
10/27/57   32921 (digitally restored)

Adjacent to Woolworth's, Sautter's Shoe Store had an attractive display. This was considered a branch of their downtown store on lower Genesee Street.
10/20/58   33177

8/21/53   30762

Utica Mutual Insurance Company constructed a showcase building on Genesee Street, past the former Utica Country Day School and opposite the junction of Route 12 with Route 5. The move into the new building was the biggest such undertaking in Utica's history.
Short concrete posts and a dirt embankment were added between the building and the street in 1959 after the driver of a tractor trailer lost control on Route 12 and smashed into the front of the building. The driver was killed but fortunately most of the workers had left the area.
3/11/54   31311 A

Work areas for everyone were pleasant and there was always plenty of work. The cafeteria was necessary with "the Mutual" so far from many lunch places.
8/53   30762 A, B & C

8/53   30762 D, E & F

The parking lot was filled to overflowing when the new P&C opened on Campion Road in New Hartford and the shoppers crowded in.
9/14/55   32082 A

9/14/55   32082 B, C

When the Grange League Federation (GLF)—later known as Agway—was looking for a site for their regional offices, they found it on Campion Road in New Hartford. The accounting department shown here was over the Aurora Bowlaway.
4/23/55   31916

Representative of many area establishments, the soda fountain at the Frankfort Diner was shining glass and gleaming stainless steel.
4/10/56   32365

Hamilton College in nearby Clinton was expanding also. Soper Commons, a landmark campus dining hall, was enlarged with a new kitchen.
7/25/58   33106

2/6/59   33367 A

The new Dunham Dormitory at Hamilton—originally for freshmen—had spacious lounges and a snack bar. It was projected to cost $1,250,000.

2/6/59   33367 B

2/6/59   33367 C

12/26/59   33466 A

Over the hill and out of sight until called for was the Waterville Crematory. Constructed by the Waterville Cemetery Association to answer the growing demand for this alternative to traditional burial, it came to serve a wide area.

12/26/59   33466 B

This is probably a copy of an earlier picture, but the Gatesdale Dairy Bar in Bridgewater still looks familiar. It was a great place to stop when out for a drive on Route 20 or a visit to the Upstate Auto Museum across the road.
10/21/54   30782

With several children in an average family, and with the move to the suburbs, family rooms became popular as second living rooms. Here Bair Advertising showed a very upscale room in an advertisement for Utica Radiator's baseboard heating units. The new television set was often placed in the family room. In 1952 an RCA 21-inch, black and white set was advertised at $339.95.
1/15/55   31761 B

Home, School and Play

While the Rhoades photographers spent most of their time in industrial or commercial settings, some assignments gave us glimpses of domestic life, education and recreation. But even these were taken for commercial purposes and have the same tidy, well composed look as the firm's other work.

With the coming of political stability and the fading of Great Depression memories, the desire for home and family was rampant in the country and the Mohawk Valley was no exception. Those who had served in World War II were more than ready to enjoy the life they had been fighting for. A home in the country with grass and flowers and trees was the ideal.

Rhoades' files recall the growth of suburbia. Acres of former farmland in North Utica and the Towns of Deerfield, Marcy, New Hartford and Whitestown were subdivided to grow new crops of Cape Cods, ranches and split-levels. Real estate developers and local manufacturers of radios, heating equipment and other home furnishings all wanted pictures.

The baby boom and the move to newer city neighborhoods and the suburbs also led to a boom in school construction. Schools took on a new, functional look, rarely more than two stories in height, often covering an acre or more and surrounded by playgrounds, athletic fields and parking lots.

Work was plentiful, the work week was shorter and there was more leisure time. The advent of radios and especially television quickly filled much of it. Many opted for sports such as bowling, softball, golf and skiing. For boys Little League baseball supplanted sandlot pickup games; this offered one advantage to historians—team pictures.

There were shadows but they were ignored rather easily. The communist threat led to air raid drills in school and some backyard bomb shelters. We had "The Bomb" but "they" had it too, so the situation was an uneasy standoff. In the dark of night we could sometimes hear long range bombers overhead, ready for instant retaliation if someone in Moscow should push the button. They were first in space with two Sputniks, but we soon caught up and had Explorer circling overhead.

These threats could be put out of mind. We reveled in prosperity. Life was good.

This 1952 reproduction of WKTV advertising art suggests the type of work that would eventually become a Rhoades stock in trade. In 1956, WKTV increased power to 31,600 watts and two years later changed to Channel 2.
5/19/52   29709

Local pantomimist and baseball clown Billy Mills performed for the WKTV camera; his act was in demand for openings and conventions.
11/51   29157 (digitally restored)

1/15/55   31761 A

Utica Radiator advertised baseboard heating units with scenes of model houses. The heating units may be new, but furniture styles belonged to an earlier time. Kitchens were bright and white.
1/15/55   31761 C

81

Two girls were learning to operate a multilith machine at the New York State School for the Deaf in Rome. These ancestors of today's copy machines were notoriously noisy.
3/14/56   32319

This class was meeting in the New Hartford High School with the girls in neat dresses (some with bobby socks) and the boys in well-pressed shirts and trimmed hair.
9/54   31659 (digitally restored)

Organized play for children was the order of the day and that included Little League baseball. In Utica, there were eight leagues and the season started with a parade. However, these teams played in the New Hartford League and houses on Bohling Road formed the backdrop.
6/3/57   32805 A

6/3/57   32805 B

Adults had organized recreation too. Here the Printing House Craftsmen gathered for a barbecue and a group picture.
8/6/51   28859 A

11/17/50   28167

With the introduction of well-lighted, spacious alleys and automatic pinsetters, bowling became a popular family sport. Here is Aurora Bowlaway in New Hartford, which opened officially May 1, 1951.
11/17/50   28170

Milo Smith, a farmer living on Shell's Bush Road in Herkimer County, created these beautiful circus models using a scale of one inch to one foot. Here they were in the window of an area jewelry store to advertise the annual Shrine Circus, eagerly anticipated by children of all ages.
10/28/55   32124

These Plymouths were ready for sale. Unfortunately, the popular colors—cream, turquoise, pink—cannot be seen, but the tail fins were beginning to sprout in these models. Together with the former Utica Fire Alarm Telegraph Company building in the background, this lot later became part of the site of the Utica Memorial Auditorium.
6/17/56   32424

Getting There

The number of automobiles increased rapidly during this period. Cars were a necessity for suburbanites, as well as for city dwellers. Long distance travel was by car or plane, to the detriment of the railroads. Within a year of the Thruway's opening, passenger traffic on the New York Central had dropped by fifty percent!

With the rising number of cars, there had to be more control of traffic. As early as 1950, left turns at Oneida Square in Utica were banned and in the first four months of 1953, forty-seven pedestrians were injured and two killed. A safety program for those on foot was started; the motto was "Be a Live Duck." In 1957, people applying for drivers' licenses had to have their vision tested; however, the results of those tests were not considered when issuing licenses.

Good roads became a popular cause and politicians who voted for them usually were elected. The New York State Thruway was hailed as a 488-mile highway with no traffic lights. A gala celebration was held at the end of October 1954; Governor Thomas E. Dewey led a motorcade from Newburgh to Utica with stops along the way for local celebrations and a banquet at the Hotel Utica.

A four-lane, limited-access "arterial" was planned to connect Route 12 at Oriskany Circle to Route 5 in New Hartford. However, construction was held up for many months over questions of pedestrian safety between Court and Noyes Streets.

On September 1, 1950, Robinson Airlines scheduled regular fights from the new Oneida County Airport. Unfortunately, five days after the first flight departed, a crash at nearby Coleman's Mills killed thirteen passengers. Despite this setback, Robinson continued and, as Mohawk Airlines, became a successful regional airline.

The York Rake Company was finishing up work on the Thruway. These shots were taken near the Route 5 bridge over the Thruway in the Town of Schuyler, just east of Utica.
6/10/54   31509 C

6/10/54   31509 D

This showroom on Lafayette Street was open after dark to serve working customers. A new Plymouth cost $2,200 to $2,500 with no options.
6/19/53   30587 G

With extensive annual restyling, the look of American cars changed dramatically in this period; compare these 1957 models with the 1953s above.
11/7/56   32413

In 1956, Mohawk Airlines—"Route of the Air Chiefs" and formerly Robinson Airlines—was seeking a new home and was welcomed at Oneida County Airport. Their fleet consisted of eleven Convairs like these and eleven DC-3s.
6/17/57   32818 A

This dramatic shot shows a DC-3 being towed from the hangar at Oneida County Airport.
6/17/ 57   32818 B

The Villages of Frankfort and New Hartford bought their Ford police cars at Dahl Motors on Elizabeth Street in Utica.
10/24/53   30896 (digitally restored)

The Frankfort Center Fire Department took delivery of this neat little "squad car" from Dahl Motors. It answered calls for first aid and accidents, transported volunteers to fires and parades and served as a firematic competition vehicle, as suggested by the team name "Ramblers" on the hood.
6/3/52   29816

The 1951 Mercury looked pretty spiffy on the showroom floor at Gordon Davis Motors, 2007 Genesee Street in Utica. Small showrooms with space for only one or two cars were common in the days before most dealers moved to larger sites on Commercial Drive or River Road.
9/11/51   28966

Where there were cars, there had to be gas stations. This was the well-stocked interior of Casaletta's in Washington Mills. No such establishment was complete without a big red Coca-Cola cooler on the floor and a pay phone on the wall.
8/13/51   28857 B

In 1962, this Sunoco station opened at 1535 York Street. Trading stamps were very popular; this station gave Triple-S Blue Stamps, one for every 10¢ spent. Pasted into books, they could be exchanged for merchandise at "stamp stores."
7/15/62   33802

With the increase in overnight travel by car, motels proved more popular than downtown hotels. The Motel Hamilton was under construction at the Thruway exit on the site of the former Braves baseball field.
8/29/56   32472

The Colonial was one of many motels to serve travellers on Route 5, east of Utica.
8/31/51   28924

All motel rooms of that period had much the same appearance. This unidentified interior was shot for Utica Motel Supply, dealers in furniture and bedding.
6/15/56   32396

Looking northwest from the roof of the International Heater Company at Park Avenue and Broad Street, the New York Central Railroad yard showed great activity. The oil storage tanks were farther away with Deerfield Hill still farther.
6/58   33103

Union Station had more than a dozen passenger tracks with platforms protected by canopies and reached through a pedestrian "subway" tunnel. Elevators lifted baggage, mail and express carts from a second tunnel to trackside.
9/29/52   30034

The Murray Warehouse at Whitesboro and Washington Streets was served by the Delaware, Lackawanna & Western after the New York, Ontario & Western ceased operations in 1957. "The Route of Phoebe Snow" referred to the DL&W's early 20th century advertising figure and a postwar streamliner of the same name.
12/4/58   33219

The rattle of glass milk bottles was a welcome wake-up sound in this period. Home delivery of milk required fleets of trucks. These classic DIVCOs (Detroit Industrial Vehicle Company) were based at the Borden's plant at Francis and Tracy Streets.
6/3/49   26224 (digitally restored)

People's Express, headquartered at 424-426 Broad Street, provided delivery service for several local furniture and department stores. Many of their trucks were specially lettered and dedicated to serving specific stores.
9/12/53   30879 B

People's Express purchased this shiny new Ford from Dahl Motors. Berger's was on Columbia Street.
5/17/51   28614

On Oriskany Boulevard, Utica Mack's home was in a distinctive building, faced with green and yellow checkerboard tiles.
9/12/53   32776

This workman was shaping the end of a tank on a large rapidly rotating wheel at the Utica Steam Engine and Boiler Works on Whitesboro Street. These tanks, of high grade stainless steel, were used for the storage of milk and milk products.
4/28/55   31920

From Loom to Boom

The 1950s started well for the area when Chicago Pneumatic announced that five hundred new people would be hired. The 1950 City Directory listed eighty-five manufacturing plants employing 43,100 people. They made cotton and woolen cloth, knit goods, rayon yarn, sheets, men's clothing, heating and ventilating equipment, springs and mattresses, luggage, sheet metal stampings, machinery, sprayers, fishing tackle, paper products, ice cream coolers, nippers, pliers and pneumatic tools.

By 1955, nearly all of the textile mills had moved south and in 1960 the city directory no longer listed cotton and woolen cloth, knit goods and sheets. Springs and mattresses and commercial refrigeration were no longer included either, but electronic products and calculating and computing machines were added. In a laudatory article in 1957, *Fortune* called Utica one of the widest awake cities on the Thruway.

General Electric operated three plants; radios for home use were made on Bleecker Street, two-way radios on Kent Street and on French Road equipment needed for the Cold War and space exploration—this in great secrecy. *Aviation Week*, a trade journal, called French Road "one of the most completely automated plants in the country." In 1956, more the 3,800 people worked there with an annual payroll greater than $16,000,000. Many of these actually worked in the former Oneita Knitting and Utica and Mohawk Cotton mills on Broad Street, spaces added when the operations expanded.

1/5/52 29255 B

In this plant at Harbor Point, soft coal was transformed into coke which was then used for the manufacture of cooking gas. With the arrival of natural gas pipelines in 1951, it was no longer needed and was about to be razed.
1/5/52 29255 C

1/5/52 29255 E

The offices of International Heater occupied this interesting building at the corner of Park Avenue and Broad Street.
9/4/52   29985 (digitally restored)

Thousands of small radios were made in the General Electric Radio Receiver plant at 1900 Bleecker Street, near Culver Avenue.
12/29/51   29233 A

2/5/52   29359

Here the radios were boxed and ready to ship.
12/29/51   29233 C

In 1956, an automatic clock radio (perhaps not this model, however) sold for $24.95.
6/22/56   32391 (digitally restored)

109

This label was the only photo connected with GE's Light Military Electronics Division to be found in the Rhoades Collection. Mum was the word.
8/54   31600

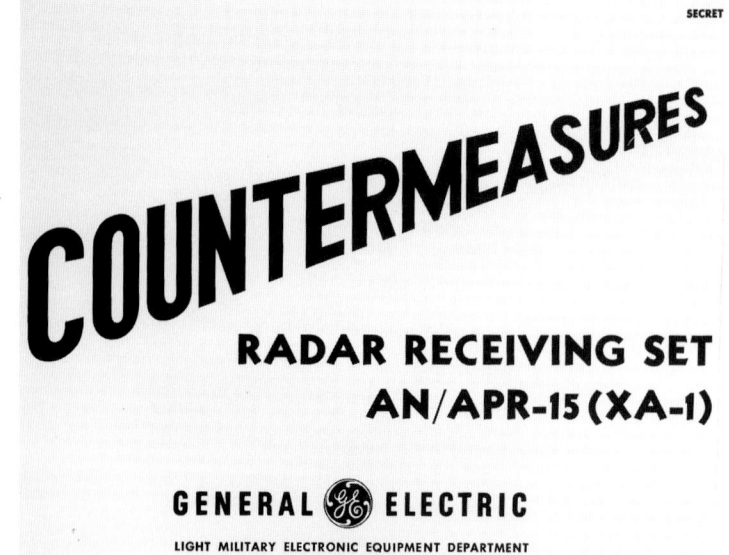

COUNTERMEASURES

RADAR RECEIVING SET
AN/APR-15 (XA-1)

GENERAL ELECTRIC

LIGHT MILITARY ELECTRONIC EQUIPMENT DEPARTMENT
FRENCH ROAD, UTICA, N.Y.

SECRET

Niagara Mohawk Power Company was installing new and impressive turbines in 1952.
6/13/52   29804

This aerial photo shows the Bendix plant—originally built for Continental Can Company on the former Wankel Playgound—on Seward Avenue. The New York Telephone garage was across the street. The small houses were on French Road and crops were grown on the open land behind the plant.
7/26/52   29879

Long knives were being honed at Utica Cutlery on a grinder made in the Munson Mill division of Divine Brothers.
10/20/55   32117

11/11/53   31051 A

Vacuum metal technology was introduced at Utica Drop Forge by Dr. Falih Darmara in 1952. The specially purified metals were several times stronger than those traditionally produced and were used in jet engines and other applications for the Air Force. Output was greatly increased when two 1,000-pound furnaces were introduced in place of one 300-pound furnace. The forerunner of Special Metals Corporation, this was the first company in the nation to achieve large scale production with vacuum induction furnaces.

11/11/53   31051 B

8/12/58   33115 A

Waterbury Felt Company in Oriskany was one of the older industries in the area. Its workers spun and wove wool into huge "felts" used in paper-making machinery. Some of the material was also made into blankets.
8/12/58   33115 B

7/21/59   33421

4/20/52   29603 A

Whitestown Trencher demonstrated the use of its equipment, probably on the sand banks along Route 69.
4/20/52   29603 B

The photographer had to go to Long Lake to get these shots of a Pettibone Mulliken log skidder—made in Rome—in action.
1/4/56   32597 A

1/4/56   32597 B

As a part of its 50th anniversary celebration, Duxbak—manufacturer of outdoor clothing—held a monthly drawing for a hunting dog. Here company officials posed with one of the prizes. Duxbak's plant was at the corner of Noyes Street and Lincoln Avenue.
11/10/55   32146

Just across Noyes Street, Utica Cutlery made stainless steel tableware in addition to knives of all kinds.
1/8/59   33252 B

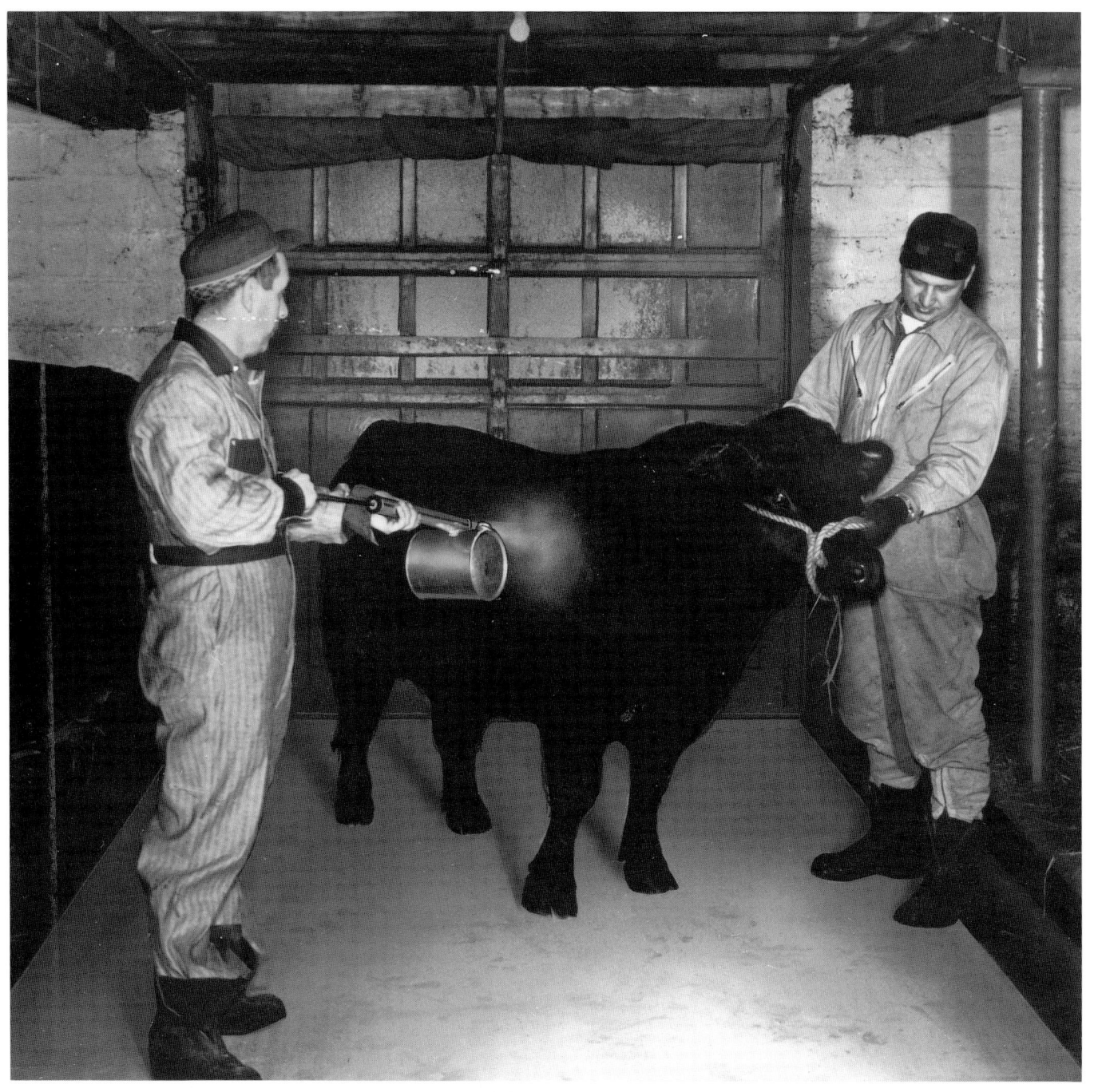

Sprayers made by D. B. Smith had many applications in industry and agriculture, including treating a bull with pesticides.
2/15/59   33256

7/13/59   33394

Partlow Corporation in New Hartford was noted for temperature control devices and instruments, for applications ranging from refrigerated trailers to duplicating machines.
7/20/59   33422

Savage Arms had turned from machine guns to peacetime products like sporting rifles, ice cream cabinets and lawn mowers but the local plant was closed and operations consolidated at Chicopee, Massachusetts in 1956. On the other side of Bleecker Street, the Chicago Pneumatic plant sprawled just over the Herkimer County line.
12/30/55   32206 (digitally restored)

This Erie forge hammer was used to form turbine blades for jet engines from aluminum bronze or titanium at Utica Drop Forge. The hot metal was shaped by the pressure of the hammer.
9/25/52   30018 H

Advertising was big business too, making one want more of everything. Moser & Cotins, with offices on Hopper Street, handled many accounts in the Mohawk Valley and beyond. Here, some of the staff was hard at work.
6/5/56   32385

Copper-bottom Revere Ware—made in nearby Rome—became a favorite of housewives and chefs coast to coast, and a popular wedding gift.
10/4/52   30054

Cartoonist J. R. Williams used his talents and characters to promote Duofold underwear, made in Mohawk. Major Hoople, the paunchy fellow with the fez, and the other residents of "Our Boarding House" were funny-page favorites as were the characters who lived "Out Our Way."

1/22/59   33250 A

One of the best-known industries in the area was the West End Brewery, the sole survivor of several smaller breweries. Here were two of the processes which made the product possible. The new brew house, completed in 1948, was so popular with visitors that the brewery decided to offer regular tours. Beginning in 1965, these became one of Utica's best-known tourist attractions.
1/22/59   33250 B

The bottling plant, where bottles rushed along conveyor belts to be filled, capped and packaged, became one of the most popular stops on the brewery tour.
10/23/51   29098

Beer companies advertised heavily and West End was no exception. In 1957, they employed traditional "cheesecake" but in 1961 tried a new tactic, using vintage photographs (or carefully staged imitations) and promoting the old-time quality of Utica Club.
6/15/57   32825

6/17/61   33682 D

The hugely popular talking steins, Schultz and Dooley, created for West End by renowned puppeteer Bill Baird, became two of Utica's most famous "citizens" and television personalities.
6/17/61   32682

Digital Retouching

Some years ago many of the negatives in the Russell Rhoades Collection were damaged when neighboring buildings burned and Rhoades' basement was flooded with water. Twenty-one badly damaged images in this collection are contained in this book. When you look at them, however, you will not see the effects of heat and water because they have been restored using techniques from the newly emerging field of digital photography. This work was painstakingly performed by Theresa Sokolowski, owner of Visual Designs in Utica, under the direction of Dr. Robert Dell, professor in the Physical Science Department at Mohawk Valley Community College. The restored images in this book were retouched using equipment in that department.

Digital photography involves converting a photographic image to a set of numbers by means of a process called "digitization." Once the image has been scanned and digitized it can be loaded into a computer where the numbers representing the image can be manipulated with the aid of special image manipulation software. Below is an example of one of the original images. The restored photo next to it is a testimony to the power of digital techniques for photo restoration, as are the other restored images in this book.

Utica's landmark old City Hall adjoined the Bank of Utica, then known as the Industrial Bank of Utica.
1/8/54   31185 (digitally restored)

Afterword

We are often asked "Why don't you publish a picture of this or that?" All too often the answer must be, "We can't publish what we don't have." Limited staff for research and nearly non-existent funds for acquisition have hampered our efforts at collecting. But all too often the reason is that the pictures in question, if they were ever taken in the first place, have yet to be donated, or have been discarded. While it is wonderful to have these photographs, at the same time it is distressing to know how much has been lost over the years, continues to be lost every day, or threatens to be lost in the future.

However, there are bright spots and the saving of the Rhoades Collection is one of the brightest. As commercial photographers, Russel Rhoades and his associates worked primarily for manufacturers, advertising agencies, insurance companies, real estate brokers and attorneys. They were not creative story-tellers, nor portrait photographers, nor architectural photographers. Their job was to present a product as favorably as possible so that someone might buy it, an accident scene as clearly as possible so that justice might be done, or a piece of artwork for the best possible reproduction.

Only with the passage of time did the Rhoades negatives come to be appreciated as historical documents. In the meantime, they were just old files in the basement. What is fortunate is that, during this precarious period of being neither new nor really old, they were simply ignored and not discarded.

Turning to the digitization process used and described in this book, this technology does provide a new tool for the restoration of damaged images. But like most great discoveries, it also has drawbacks. Digitization makes possible unprecedented manipulation of photographic images, virtually undetectable, unlike earlier crude cut-and-paste methods.

Manipulation of photographs is nothing new. Early twentieth century postcard pictures were heavily retouched, and one need look no farther than the Society's own collection to compare original negatives with finished postcards from which distracting utility poles and wires, litter, and even people have been conveniently removed. It is clear from the negatives that "the good old days" were not nearly so neat and tidy as the postcard publishers would have had us believe.

The new technology offers both opportunities and challenges to archivists. Digitization and the placement of images onto computer discs is proving a boon to major photographic repositories and is already spreading to local historical societies. Video-disc images, coupled with computer data bases, can greatly facilitate research in photographic archives, all the while protecting vulnerable negatives and other original materials from theft, damage or simple wear and tear.

—*Doug Preston*

Copies of the photographs in this book, and in other collections of the Society are available by special order. For further information, contact the Society at 1608 Genesee Street, Utica, New York 13502, or call 315-735-3642.